Latin American Economic Development

D0949282

Latin America is one of the most interesting parts of the world. The region's illustrious history, culture, and geography are famous internationally, but in terms of economics, Latin America has been generally associated with problems. For many, the combination of a resource-rich region and poor economic conditions has been a puzzle. *Latin American Economic Development* provides the most up-to-date exploration of how this happened with a focus on why the continent can be considered to have underperformed, how the various Latin American economies function, and the future prospects for the region.

This textbook addresses the economic problems of Latin America theme by theme. The first four centuries of Latin American economic development are explained with reference to historical and institutional factors; the role of commodities; import substitution industrialization; and the resultant slow growth of the region. The development of Latin America during the twentieth century is examined through the policies of governments toward international trade and the management of the exchange rate. These policies lead to the accumulation of significant debt in the region that resulted in substantial economic instability. The final section of the book explains how all of these themes have contributed to two dominant problems for the region: poverty and inequality.

The purpose of this book is to provide a comprehensive text for increasingly popular undergraduate economics courses on Latin America. However, the book has been carefully designed for use by both students majoring in economics and for those in other disciplines looking for a wide-ranging guide to the region. This book should be an invaluable resource for undergraduates looking at Latin American economics, growth, and development.

Javier A. Reyes is an Associate Professor of Economics in the Economics Department of the Sam M. Walton College of Business at the University of Arkansas, USA.

W. Charles Sawyer is the Hal Wright Professor of Latin American Economics at Texas Christian University, USA.

Latin American Economic Development

Javier A. Reyes and W. Charles Sawyer

 Routledge
Taylor & Francis Group

LONDON AND NEW YORK

First published 2011
by Routledge
2 Park Square, Milton Park, Abingdon, Oxon OX14 4RN

Simultaneously published in the USA and Canada
by Routledge
711 Third Avenue, New York, NY 10017

*Routledge is an imprint of the Taylor & Francis Group,
an informa business*

Typeset in Times New Roman by Sunrise Setting Ltd, Torquay, UK

British Library Cataloguing in Publication Data
A catalogue record for this book is available
from the British Library

Library of Congress Cataloging in Publication Data
Reyes, Javier A.
Latin American economic development / by Javier A. Reyes and
W. Charles Sawyer.
p. cm.

Includes bibliographical references and index.
   1. Latin America—Economic conditions—1982
   2. Latin America—Economic policy.
      I. Sawyer, W. Charles.
      II. Title.
HC125.R4834 2010
338.98—dc22
2010037782

ISBN: 978-0-415-48613-2 (hbk)
ISBN: 978-0-415-49733-6 (pbk)
ISBN: 978-0-203-82932-5 (ebk)